AF478410

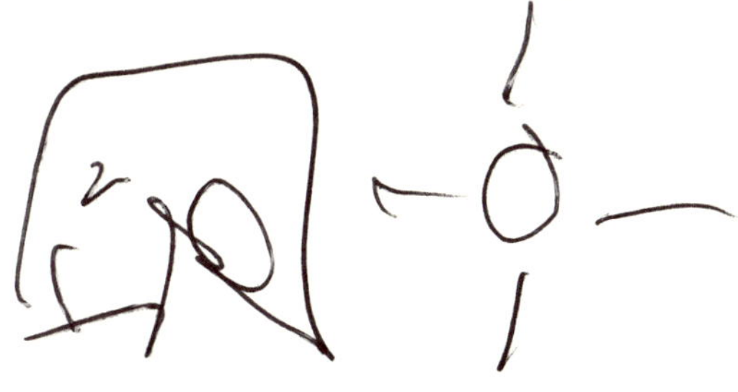

ELEGY FOR MY
BEAT GENERATION

NEELI CHERKOVSKI

LITHIC PRESS
FRUITA, COLORADO

ELEGY FOR MY BEAT GENERATION
Copyright © 2018 NEELI CHERKOVSKI
All rights reserved.

Thank you to the following journals and publications for taking some of
this work: *Big Scream, Cafe Review, Maintenance, Or,* and *Talisman (44).*

"Hydra Waterfront" and "For Agneta Falk" appeared in
Neeli Cherkovski's previous collection, *The Crow and I.*

Design & layout by Kyle Harvey.

ELEGY FOR MY BEAT GENERATION
NEELI CHERKOVSKI
ISBN 978-0-9975017-9-7
Lithic Press

for Jesse Cabrera

CONTENTS

Biography

Bibliography

ELEGY FOR MY
BEAT GENERATION

WHAT DID IT MEAN?

in memory of Gregory Corso

1

how does it mean
in the childhood of human suffering alone
on the arroyo, quick to hear a twig snap,
a pocketful of wolves huddled in a circle, the wild stallion
        etched into limestone

    four deer fording the river

liquid religion, time's timid glance
time's final trick, who invented mankind?

    your guess, amigo, on stone-sodden paths
            along narrow streets
                it was and is
        life went and came again, you see
on one side of your brain the figure of a monster
    in human clothing ranting until the words burn
            on a pile of other words
                    in a courtyard guarded by uniformed librarians

2

        it meant the perfection of your rights
                as a person in making a dream,
    or the idea of perfection, it means
something in the cosmic republic
of star systems, it meant you awaken on an
ordinary morning dressed in antelope skin

        palm trees linger like wise old men
    in long brown robes, the true mirth rises, the wind is handsome
and filled with promise, it brings
            primrose and fabulous lions
                who roar like automobile mechanics
            yeah, you have to sit for coffee

off the highway at five in the morning
when the mastodons file in
and the waitress is made of granite, so it means

so it meant, so you meet your body
in free parcels of cloud set
against the distant range, luminous shade falls
on your shoulders, it means sweet wood and incisions
                    on the wood's surface

3

        it meant breathing in a new form, the amusing
                and artful freedom to soar and become
                    somehow more than a selfish
                        soul, to share words
            to make them larger than a page
                it meant the ribbon and
stack of paper, a manual
typewriter, quite an invention
situated on a desk, or a pen in hand writhing
through winter's demonic set

4

it meant knowing things
without possessing them,
it meant the plants are not
always a commodity,
it meant/it means how you see from the depth
            inside of your
        autonomous empire of sound and sight

    rabbit warrens

fields of grain, uncrowned king of crows

it means you feel alright
on a sling of rain
        when the view from the coffee house
        depends on telephone lines

and lonely men in Chevrolets passing
   on their way to the Korean Peninsula

5

      it meant you mean
            something on this
                  meaningless planet

because you are in and out so fast
you have only words
to use, it means tapping
on the typewriter, air conditioning
sputtering, fat landlord at the door pounding

you are busy eating a plate of epic poems

why worry about the rent when you are plotting
with Ms. Emily to overthrow stupidity

down your poems
      life escaping
                  noose tightening
   little odd moon beaming
what immense silences
men may have seen
when thinking
of loud presentations
on an Aeolian harp
      under signs and symbols
            men didn't create
                  but felt through instinct
      and spontaneous hymns

BEAT DREAMS

I don't know if you understand
how it feels to feed the roots and thistles
and honeybees and you witness
the wrenched beauty of clouds
turning forever into red-hot vomit

Arabesque melting
on the streets
Pompeii's people
burnt to a shell, auras
printed on stone, music from
white branches sifting

do you recall when Mona Lisa
spoke her final words? oh she whispers
in my ear, David looked angelic
dressed in marble, chipped face pointed
toward the floor? He smiles

I never understood
the groping wound in my head
grunting, blinking at the sun
hiding from the moon's cruelty

books filled with fortune and
catastrophe, golden ass
and red pony, wide-eyed
donkey, also Geoffrey the Cat

down into the body
candlelight as guide
through glass tunnel
where benevolence
and violence join hands

into a mirror
that cracks, over to the banks
of a river, poisoned

the donkey nibbles
on grass, in his eyes corridors
of song, a mandolin offers plaintive
cries, the cops come out of their hiding
place to murder Federico

bring a single yellow petal
from the rose to place on an altar
by Moorish gate
as red ants thrive

beloved single petal
is what I wish to love
if only I knew how to
love such a thing

I might be able to
make my way
to a carpet of silt

I come onto the terrace
late at night to witness
the beginning of the end
and it is beautiful,
lava pours over the rim
of the volcano facing our room

I shake you and say "Hey,
come look at this..."
every detail perishes, a desperate sonata
gains power by repetition

random are these dreams, though
the volcano is a fact of life
born without permission, a powerful
and all-consuming thing

NOVEMBER 4

last night I met a poet,
forty-two, he has dark brown eyes
and a blond mustache, no taller
than I am, wearing faded Levi's
and running shoes
two decades younger, facing the images
and jostles with the bellicose populace
surrounding him, he lives
on a block of Vietnamese
restaurants and bars filled with would-be
hunters, the taste of stale beer
is on his tongue, he turns
pages of my book,

with poetry no one is quite sure, they sit in a corner
aware of human ceremonies
to ask: "Did you really know Walt Whitman?"

November 4, I'm trying to push incest aside,
November is a cobra, travail gathers,
I unfold morning's news to find nothing
of interest, instead I take inventory of that
poet's coat, of his trousers, of his way of holding mocha

he worked in a bookstore but was laid off, charming
to know people still work in such places

today I rake leaves and put them in
our green bin, today I drive to watch ocean waves
and low-lying fog, I look back
on broken things

November 4, news is stale beer, I knew
bartenders with sad, dog-like eyes who read
Greek and Latin philosophy,
I had friends who were married then
quickly divorced, they are

dead or old, I have friends who sit
in cafes, book in hand

November 4, I think of
the younger poet, only
last night he called, we met in Phil's Cafe,
he handed me *The Hunger Season,* a book
of poems, "men with bellies
and baseball caps stand smoking outside
of Café Nirvana," he writes in one of the poems

I love reading, "men with beer bellies
turning to the blizzard
in silent meditation," daylight
draws near, early November

men and women crowd balustrades,
leaves fall, crush them
underfoot, hear them crackle
in a cool, crisp climate, eucalyptus brightens
sycamore turns ecstatic

weather will shift dramatically
I'm thinking of changing my life,
hoping to live on, clinging to ideas, talking
to an entire chorus of writers, young and old,
and to people who know the haunts, of men
alone in cheap hotels, Old Whitman is
tricking himself, testing the water of love, lying
in wait for night to come, he is Poe, strong and
Medieval, a Modernist in his time,

fine month of lost opportunity
may grand ambition reign,
the prophet ran to roll a joint,
Twin Towers collapsed,
Buddha dynamited
twice in November

in "Balloons" the younger poet begins:
"It is Tuesday, September 4
two thousand and seven..."

In "Spider Man" he writes:
"The walls are fucking
and the doors are bleeding
over this November afternoon..."

NO MOON

not anymore will I hold
an image of the moon, no moon anymore

I wanted to love you bathed
in lunar night closed by insanity

provided by space and mortality
I needed you that way long ago

heroic fathers dead, no more
moon, not one single fit of it, not in the midst

of a mirror or in garden glass, no moonlight tune
rolling in, though the snarl on my need

coiled round, you slept in the next room
for two years or maybe I was mistaken

the demonic ghost had taken your place,
you are blameless, I am at fault, you could've loved me

in that manner, to tell the truth
it's difficult to love glass, to love a smooth ruby

to serve or love the self, just empty, only envy,
only a thought where lunatic bodies

sputter out, so it must be, a map of god in
my pocket, a speck of moon under the closet

clutter, moths spinning out of control, stay
stand, stoop or bow, this dancing

no moon, no second, not a half an acre, no
darkened pond, not hope, no more

I'm never alone in any way, the boys downtown
crowd into me, I hate the moon, it is not wanted

here when I sleep, not needed as we roll dice
and cut the deck, I remember how

we played with the sun, our cat, Boots, came
prancing in, she purred like crazy from the center

of light, still I hear her, then to the alley
I'd wander alone, love is not a bluff to warring

words, big red men passing, I hated sky cow
even then, ancient mounds of happiness

forever underground, what cures men
is the very impulse that makes me sick at heart

EUREKA

                ten difficult blocks
            to the subway that'll deliver us to Brooklyn,

            it is 9 p. m. – we're tired from a full day

I conjure up *Eureka*, what did Edgar Allen Poe
think? critics hated *Eureka*. even his
best friends mocked

a shattered bit of evidence disappears

I fall for the process –
                every night plague shouts

                impossible not to imagine
    what might take place on a lonesome hillside
in Nevada

    the entire cosmos fraught with mistakes

    Poe writing a guessing-game, living
    poetic freedom

        blame it on the big bang

who do you blame for Brooklyn?

for the Manhattan Bridge? for
            old book dealer's
        wise men
who knew the value
        of certain editions?

it happened, the younger man led us along
drab dark boulevards
until our joints ached
    in underground vaults

we caught one last glance
of foreboding facades

I read poems in Woodstock, and
on Vanderbilt Avenue,
and on the Lower East Side
    with Alan, Yuko, and Steve,
  we sweated cheap pizza,
    I met elderly bohemians
        weavers from Yonkers greeted me

in Woodstock we sat around a campfire
  listening to crackling wood

  under the stars
      while standing on a folding chair
I remembered cold solitude
    Poe's integrity in staying the course,
discovering creation

    whatever happens only goes by once

    Woodstock had a surplus of birds,
so many types, and, at night, perfect places
    to stumble, Raymond held my arm
        on the steps of an ancient Hindu temple,
      he put me in bed
  upstairs, Jesse beside me, I read from the Odes:
"a ploughman, a field of strawberries…"

    I made fifty-five dollars and dreamed
of spending it, Peter liked my poems, we had both
grown old

    while visiting Woodstock we passed the placid lake,
      then drove by the Karmapa's compound,
I nearly died when a God-like youth sat
at the piano while the hummingbird
  ordered coffee

the subway delivers Grand Army Concourse
        near Matt's house on a leaf-ridden street
    around the corner from burial mound gratitude
and the delicatessen, just south of Eureka

        in an imperfect universe

ONE LAST MIND

for Q. R. Hand

one last mind
Q. R., only he remembers
depot Manhattan
his arms crossed
on bearded town
around moonlight's glitter
such as he told when old enough to notice
it's the poet, one more morning
in step

the world wings him
yet he bounces
caught in spirit, ecstatic places
between words
a drum, the bass, quick and subtle
silence bound
remains eye to eye
riffing through muted bee bop
drawn north further, must be Hand's
ancient room
never enough beat
he talks to sweet hipsters
on sweeping lanes
I'd find him
Saturday morning, dread leaves
cover his feet, he pushes up from the Blues
to riggings over a black fire
kindly move alongside the stream

he invokes pretty decades
roundabout, how are you doing?
I'd follow bright November
into solitude, blue mast swaying
grip chords
over beatific grid of humane flute

throngs of light up from the mighty Mississippi
and onto Mission Street
where mist filters fragile beads, flowers
alongside bumble bees, city bees
bouncing, stopping for coffee
Q. R. baseball bread whack
splinter of bat flies off
ten thousand images lash out for
Coltrane – additional sounds
where Hand
comes up to the mound –
he smiles when he hits it out of the park

ON THE DAY ALLEN DIED

on the day Allen died
I saw a green truck
in the sky and read
his supermarket poem
where naughty Walt Whitman
eyes the grocery boys

now it is four centuries
since Allen detonated
taking a tambourine
and the dimmed outline
of beautiful travelers

good old Allen
sitting on a chair
way up in the sky
reading poems
to Philip the Bear

you'd think the world
existed for creation and
forward motion, you
hop a subway train
find yourself on a bleak
sidewalk in the rain
trying not
to be frightened
or completely insane

you follow Allen
into the dark hole
of a dime store
poke around, he's
talking to a crusty
hipster by the
Coca-Cola machine

The largest moon
in the world hovered
over Allen's head,

when he died
we thought maybe
we've lost some
of our spirit, we
said goodbye
to American rebellion
and gone on
to other scenes

on the day he died
the pensive truths
were ever more rooted

we knew the poet
was a marvelous disgrace
just as we all are
in our way, he
praised carnations
this King of the May
in communist Prague 1965

we admire ourselves anyway
in our silly hats, in
wintry somber bedrooms
trying to wring some snow
out of emptiness
in order to believe
one more time if for
no other reason...

on the day Allen died
I was surprised
to find a drop
of grace flying

in my face, I said
the elusive monarch
will return
to rule
because the poet
lay in bed surrounded by
the rise and fall of mortal light
he closed his eyes
and everything was fine

POETRY AND SUCCESS

do you understand why
she came running into the
basement dumb ochre
paintings hung upside down

what did she expect
success, or what? does anyone
dare imagine in wicked
hours a poem

was designed to explain
anything? – a poem
explains nothing –
meant to be primitive

comment on process,
you may ask, what process?
the poem is a twitter of inner
mind, a financial burden

unless you are handsome
and know how to win awards
and garner accolades, but in truth
poesy acts as a cover

for success, yep
poetry is a cross dresser,
drag queen, the poem is a massive
pile of paper, the poem is askew

on cumulus or prancing on ozone
or falling like a leaf or blowing in
the breeze or escaping from a prison
cell or hanging by a noose

you must understand, I beg you
to understand you need to go under
the skin of it, to put your fingers
around it, stop explaining, you are

already dressed for success, Dylan
Thomas drank his poems to death
in the White Horse Tavern, Robert
Frost saw the dark oak and

blesses us, and so on and so on
guess who comes next?
poetry is raw power,
a ticket for success

so let her run and trip –
if the basement floods
so fucking what – she owns it –
she understands

PAPERS

all over my generation
a few cardboard boxes of the high and low
stacked in a closet
behind bookshelves
a misery of papers to load
when the time comes
they whisper fake views – shame
shame when I was thirteen listening to
gutter rats, other boys loved baseball
asinine genius boys smirking
so that one day they'd run law firms like G. D.
who served a large corporation
I saw his business squirming in class
foul mind of a teacher's narrow truth
which might as well be Sunday's editorial
ten boxes of stuff
three boxes of trees
flowers mostly roses how many times
can you get away with that?
roads, rows of spoons, a tow truck
tough luck, papers are a mess
smears of ink, bad printer makes black spots
wrinkled eyes, rubber siding the lines sprint
I got into this generation by lying
and wearing a mask, first a jaguar
with gold earrings, then a black cat white paws,
then they dressed me like a girl ruby red lipstick,
I hid behind Red Riding Hood until she died,
my papers oh the thick weight they are,
like concrete sidewalk where homeless folks
defecate, we need to unmask
the words to understand Yosemite, we must
scale snow-capped mountains
on our way across the Bay

**

only then we have our say, we light votive sticks
for those who labor under wisdom, who haunt
abandoned storm drains, witness ludicrous
low mind sound tracks
yet survive, we don't worry no more worry, no dumb
no we, does not matter, oh way, what changes
reminds us relics await, my papers
are true lily pads,
I invented performers and artists
and put them into cardboard boxes,
boxes came from OfficeMax
appear strong enough to survive transport
to the somber library, on the first page
of my papers I see an airplane crash into a tree
long ago, 1953, I was eight
plane made of masking tape
the lady got out flipped her six shooter until
she hit the bulls-eye, we applauded
my papers make me smile
because I'm an enemy to the ruthless
and artless, but am a liar as well,
I don't like flags or living under dead-weight

paper I like, clear white sheets of dread adorn
even dark spaces, closet soon empty,
door open, librarians do not
refuse my generation, my friend and
neighbor, the poets I admire most do not
change, they grow ancient, not old

SHE LIKES ME

she like me
despite this garland
of snapdragons
from heaven

she heard the song
of idiots,
preferring tones
of fat Winter night

her eyes had seen men
of the barricades
and recorded everything
from her chamber

she fell very ill
when Eve wore
a blood-drenched face
on beautiful wings

she didn't like
when I placed
forget-me-nots
on mud-drenched roads

I found agates and
driftwood, shells lay
everywhere, some
had purple throats

she sailed past
a cloud, telling me
to sit still, "comb your
hair," did she not know

creation is wild poverty,
she would say, "prove it,"
but I simply explained
agate to sea gulls

waste no spite. I
hid by the spinning vapor
of sea grass in tufts
on nearby dunes

and praised the future
wise ones who would
undertake an exploration
of sound and form

ONE ROAD

for Jack Hirschman

easy going...
tumbleweed gasoline pound earth
eyeless rattle of train engine roaring
drowning skies in suburban Colorado

huge men eating three-egg omelets
or steaks the size of Rhode Island

please pass the aggression –
some version of Albert Einstein
suddenly awakened by rattlesnakes
as midnight approaches

vehement cries of cosmos raptor rapture rupture
jumping borders, hydrogen bomb attached
to a song of copper pennies

**

we walk into Barnes and Noble Bookstore,
hands tied behind our backs, nice folk
drinking coffee at the Starbuck's kiosk

they don't stock *Sometimes A Great Notion*
but she offers turtle dove
I am informed

I always thought Socrates was a saint and that he waits
in back of the bookstore

lift earth over red spirit
may blinking bloom touch a bookcase,
kick the Bible Belt,
I do not need you anymore.
out the door

we get up in the morning
for beaver dam, beavers chew wood
and make nifty dams
then comes Danny to carry off the wood
he gives me a walking stick, I trek quickly
through towns like Winnemucca and Elko
walking astride the Colorado River
to join the cast of lonesome dove
in the middle of nowhere

**

Ah, you rip the chord here,
we came by rail,
I pace the aisle

comes Peter Cottontail
to stir folk, you'd rewrite an American tragedy
on avenues of heartland cities

me!! it's me again!!
Oh, just when I thought all sense of self
had vanished

I tried writing about jackrabbits and
sage and the dinosaur cliffs before you reach
Grand Junction

**

bleak road – fleet road
roll of nurses as wide as bison

"Stella, would you please feed the animals
afore it get so dark that an owl won't hoot
for a damn plugged nickel"
she is in the emergency room
eating fresh-baked cookies

**

I came east without toothbrush
or a tube of toothpaste
my love is for lyrical didactic luminosity
splashed onto Dharma dreams
released on this rambled terrain

like in parts of JOB where the sons of God
park their cars and drink whiskey

now we are doomed to escape
"Ancestors of Everything"

including abandonment of poesy
by Rimbaud before the age of 20

**

because my pal
disembodied soon
on a magic carpet of wicked whacky shades
floating over night
in pain, I greet cattle and come to dream
like a patient monk

my Lord is more than a master craftsman
he is a breeze, team up with him
as you dare waves on a lonely stretch
forget the will to overcome
because I place a hand
at the designated moment to say goodbye
to fading Levi's of my creator

I think on him as one of the sons
of all-encompassing perfection

FOR A FRIEND FAR AWAY

the storm front said don't bother
waiting for buckets of rain, ignore thunder
rising in the ancient brain, jump synapses
for glory implicit in strong weather,
continue talking humankind,
embrace selfish concern for plots of vegetables

shortness of breath will build a scheme
to kill enemies, make a yellow poinsettia
for spaces down the hallway

proceed in blind adoration, go ahead and rage,
put mud on your head like a cranky child
who does not get his way
and throws his toy airplane
onto the floor,
he sulks and wanders into the empty quarter

I approach the storm front
wearing aged black tunic my uncle gave
long ago in his studio, he knew I was a child
of pigment and palette,
now I frown for tides secured by fantasy,
I salute Satanic mother
for her hierarchies of sound

I please invisible forms
rising out of Baroque musings on the radio
as I barrel down the highway

find me in the coffee house
with my friend who died because he drank a taxicab
and fell into the rabbit hole to dine
with the Queen of Art at her long, oaken table

I love compatriots
who go insane praising martyred poets
whilst I seem to be a disc of jade
on doldrums, a ribbon of snow
on the spine of an obelisk

tell the philosopher to write more poems –
send them to my address in Pine Cone City,
I will cherish graphic light, pin hopes
on the mirroring of man in nature
and nature on its own two feet

I'm not talking dualism,
no, it's bow and arrow wielded, one intention
to forward,
I learned this from a master
who turns gold into aluminum
and lives in a trailer by the abandoned ski slope
on the outskirts of Running Springs

NO GOING HOME

all those dumb years
are just dumb,
the poster boards and
cheap plaster, wobbly chairs
dirty floors
all we can think of
is not going home

what we imagine
is how we will never
go home
not even when we slam
the door shut
on acres of light and shadow

I have no son or daughter
to mourn a hillside of dying redwood trees
but I will go anyway
and not go home on the way

no one will go with me
to the darkness

I will not go home

no one will offer a red rose stem
for my lips

I will resist any force
trying to bring me home

it's difficult to believe
any of us will forever fly

I hope for sorrows of stop and go
on mountain tops where bighorn
spend their days, if they can perish
my identity may vanish

I saw an aged prophet
out on the corner

I saw my father
take a final fling
and perish in the twinkle of an eye

then why shouldn't I
go that way?

I will tumble through the hole
but never to caress frail stalk
of the fig tree my father
watered diligently until it drowned

rotting peaches
we could not save, every year

I will not go home

LAST TIME

last time lost mind found a sign
to patch divided path
one way to purgatorial splendor
the other leads who knows
a ghost perhaps leads late luck
in the forest an owl drenching
downpour hooded pine cold stone
oak sumac dead end, hooks
of spite, spin a dime, hood the
falcon, fake punts, cross line
hide in bushes, sky
breaks out in a sweat, what new
magnificence erupts, volcanic mind rushing
alongside melodious limb, the
tree has been in trouble ever since
sapling-hood, rush to judgment, bold
capillaries rise beyond sparkling
surface of the lake,
undertake this journey
to the last old-growth woods

famous demonic wizard fingers so
simple letting go, gray afternoon
guest book on the autobahn

we fall into lunacy, great stars, lonesome
castles, 90 miles per hour, a sigh,
careless bugler, we awaken blind

MUSE

for Kaye McDonough

deposed muse
please return
to this all-night store
for supplies you desire

engage
choosing milk, beer
smokes, candy, fame
or anonymity

you go outside
to take a leak because the toilet
is flooded do not worry
this is a small town

barbarians rule, people see
you have few teeth
shabby shoes, you loved
those beatniks who hit the trail

in beautiful weather, never looked
back, noble George, Raymond
Huckleberry Finn, drunken Poe
holding an agate lamp

Edna St. Vincent Millay
wrote "Second April,"
Langston Hughes covered
your ass when you mistook a dollar

for a twenty, sure,
it's not easy,
nobody loves us
they scold, though

we hold a fragile vessel
filled with holy water
from the insane prophet
who lives down south

sees what no one else
can see, stumble, bag in arms,
through the night of
patriotic lust

the bag rips, two peaches
roll, peanut butter jar cracks,
dog snarls from an enclave,
lose the keys

be a bear, septuagenarian
stooge, silent magician, solemn
pagan, forever pianist as night
sweetens the road

keys are safely in hand
night closes in,
hear the engine purr, drive
into darkness unfolding

nature's most imperfect pose

BE ONE

for Diane di Prima

just be one before
way back then, be clear
when Percy's skylark bangs a drum
be strong as lanterns
on strings –
hearts are in jeopardy

mingle by the crowded station
finding everyone in a hurry
to board their train, it must be true
this talk of migratory life,
it must be real, mounting legal fees,
we need to be endurable, branches swing
on bejeweled forms, eyes smiled when I
fell to my knees before dawn's glow
a moth trapped our deepest dreams
in stale air of the warehouse

wilderness gave everything
for a flicker now words split open

I devour a juicy watermelon slice

we screw people into light sockets
so they'll burn in a matter of minutes

there's an ivory stiletto
in our hearts
oh we are positive
justice cannot be served
this planet devours itself
beyond the gold screen

the bowl of chrysanthemums
turns into a fistful of knives
hot and arrogant people cram

into a cubicle and are
starved to death

I got hurt, someone screwed me
I sleep beside a man all these years
and don't know how to turn around

facing a light down-pour
I seem to walk in the aspen grove
and come to meadowland
mid-October

oh paradise stumble and rumble
in the workings of a clock, little
tithe of clock I wonder
if a star would tick away

be a bell ringer and sleep
where bodies lay

you were a villanelle
at the lunatic asylum visiting gramps
who spoke of Homeric aspirations
and the typography
of man in troubled times

ZOO

they walk to the wharf
one by one
past bank and naval academy
multitudes
who have finished exchanging money
on the black market

I think of them as phantoms
they proceed
and myself an intruder

a scarecrow passes
throwback to the baby universe
screams like the man on a bridge

the naval academy
an overwhelming catastrophe
covered in soot, banks filled
with mannequins

over by the food kiosk
majestic women brandish
poles, they swing them over heads
of the crowd, bells resound

behind a barbed wire fence
the postman and his disciple
are delivering death threats:
"Have you heard the good news?"

watch out for the news,
if you are smart you'll hide
in the shadows or rent a cabin
on a mountainside,
up a rough, narrow road.

MERCY

stones are said to speak
when auditors have left the room
they have much to say
because liberty suddenly reigns

at the end of our time
on earth the hills
will have even more to say
you may be sure, it is natural

you wonder how much does it take
to be poor, to be wealthy
or wise, how much to pitch a tent
on filthy city corners

to stand against sin,
or turn eyes away
from aged stand
of evergreens when noon abides

imagine gasping
for breath, nuggets of gold
not talking, hiding their
information quite adequately

I want to help crude men
dine in freedom's lime
on a twig, see them hop on crust
where water meets drought

mercy is acceptable,
begin with selfhood,
proceed, expect no help
from the scrim

or from silent breezes –
if you are in the doldrums
come visit, we have a sun-
drenched deck, we endure

GARDEN ELEGY

I have found the garden
sufficient today,
you are my guest
for the afternoon

I'll make strong
espresso and guide Krishna
through flowers
that flourish here

you may touch
the head of
a weathered clown
and pick jasmine

I'll reveal a waterfall
next to the mill, after
coffee one glass of wine
on the lower terrace

cactus glows,
tree fern aches
banana tree follows
sentient desire

alone at night
I follow the trail
to bamboo grove
and pray like a believer

to no specific God.

BUKOWSKI ON THE YOUNG CHERKOVSKI

'The big breasted whores shrivel away
into nothingness, and Neeli, the
still young remains neglected."

at 71 where do I stand?
two walking sticks
and one cane keep the empire
at bay

still a sense of satisfaction,
smug belief in the future
of coincidence and plain old survival

"it's about time Neeli is heard,"
proclaimed the ancient lizard

hotshots dining in Malibu
while surrealism dies
an unwanted carnation
in the yard of a retired rhinocerous

there are chambers in every pilgrim's heart
craving attention, city lights a gleam for others

"Neeli laughs at himself
on the way out the door"

I raked the leaves
in our garden and paused
to enter the catacombs
where my mentor presides
over a choir of rats

Hank says, "Neeli, come join me,
I am still lacing the gloves
and dying for light"

SPENT SHADOW

for David Meltzer

only the other day one of the great men
whispered, "languages are cormorants
at Point Mendocino"

into the demonic quilt
they stand like military police
and fight their way to the parade ground

language is a logarithm hurtled from outer space

my boyfriend is invention
if I go blind he will see for both of us

when I touch him the juniper trembles
when I kiss him a shadow bends
in time for a flotilla of words to appear

languages are real
they have spines and elbows

languages are not docile

*

joy jumps a white fence
north of the city
these eyes are shut at jetty's end
and trace the flight of a hawk

when I praise you – land rises
our passage through it rattles

when I stop at the roadside rest with truckers
and smiling families solitude hovers

groundskeeper turns on the sprinkling system
a dog barks at water's edge
paper cups lie on the ground

24 miles to Mission Soledad
on the back road
much closer is a correctional facility

language, language, language
solitude soulmate when I talk to the gods
trees listen, grass pleads for rain clouds

the mind is an ark looking for a path
along sand-driven slopes, the sound
of burnt logs in the campground

the highway patrol officer
perched at roadside

across the ocean people speak
their native tongue
and shake the gourd

a man with a tambourine chooses life
he walks with man animal

language enraptures his brain
he enjoys flute and drum

from the horde he flees
and for the vineyards a glass is raised

shape a letter onto rays of the sun
draw back from spent shadows
the rocks are rough and do not speak

twilight is not quite dark enough
but when it is "spent" we see
luminous withered light
                    "a lume spento"

don't screw with language
fill the tank and be happy
take a leak before you drive away

lone bird of prey, falcon
caught on wise windward ditty

my shoe laces are untied
and I fall to the pavement, damn!

who owns the water rights
to the bluff where I walk Orion?

HOTEL WENTLEY

a crumbling corner
of wall plaster – shadow
faint light bounces over crumbled pages
of a notebook propped against
the window, guess who waits on us,
who waits on all men? John
I do feel you are walking
into the hallway where your mind
portfolios possible routes
good endings beautiful routines

*

perhaps only one teacher survives from
those days when fog settled early

old men cough behind closed doors
dip their fingers in caffeine

*

John Joseph Wieners
arrived in town to find angelic beads hidden
in the pale color of a lamp on the famous porch
of smoke and electricity,
I remember when he first entered
that small room and gently fell

out the window – go on the alleyways
and bus journeys and provinces
of responsibility

I learn how to tie knots
that will last over time
as John faces radiance
in the *Hotel Wentley Poems*

A POEM FOR GARY SNYDER

even Han Shan
said it is better
to wait for courageous forest saints
before crossing the wasteland

forget regret
talk to the heavenly
brother

there are spaces
of note such as when the cortege
comes out of the tree
with four former presidents
led by the present one

the dead man
lies in his coffin
draped in our flag
of desperation

no time to waste
says the sentient one
who extends
both arms
in order to hold onto
compassion as if it were fruit
in a bowl

FERLINGHETTI AT 97

strolling down Columbus Avenue
to Little Joe's Restaurant
where we'd sit right before the flames
Lawrence in Greek sailor cap, beret folded in my pocket

this is 1975, there will be heavy rain
soon enough, Maria takes orders for lamb chops
the older cook will soon retire and return home to Italy

he places his cook's palm over one burner
high enough not to burn himself, flames rise
Lawrence breaks into a smile
and turns the decades into a sentiment of words
that ring across San Francisco Bay
out to the open sea

"Ferlinghetti," a woman says
and he answers, "No, I'm his twin brother –
the real one is at the bookstore
hiding behind a secret door"

the lights go on way up on Walt Whitman's cloud
where he continues to dispense wisdom
and sleights-of-hand while we eat

later we are walking again
and he hands me the keys to his Bixby cabin
"No coffee house there," he grins
"You have to make hobo coffee over the fire
in the open pit"

then he is 97 years old, still the golden glow
of a man who landed at Normandy
and surveyed the fields of Nagasaki

still he wanders the streets
near Notre Dame and hides out in Mexico
and asks Apollinaire to join us

the French poet shows up
forty-one years later and takes a seat
in what is now a Mycenaean dining room
where Edgar Allen Poe coaxes a raven from the woods

A Coney Island of the Mind was one of the books
I used to hide underneath a school notebook

Lawrence is 97 – the USA is a few decades older
it is 2016 and we need poesy
more than ever in the heartless void
that has settled

yeah, we offer gratitude if only for the cabin
and City Lights
easily as massive as the Borges library
"The Library of Babel"

endless lunch, endless fire

ENVY – AN ELEGY

envy is a flower in bloom
on this languid day in March
after rain – dahlias
have gone mad, people
embrace restless air, tendrils reach
across the heart,
citizens dine on greed
and cast wary eyes
toward Elysian fields

eyes fill with images of torture,
the collective soul trampled by armored cars,
envy cuts deep, it is difficult to sleep
once we hear the voices

I sit in the garden thinking
nothing more than this, leaves
and branches, fences and hoses, flies
and a hummingbird, wire chair

what luminosity, perhaps
in some other garden one would find
statuary, a chapel, four orange trees
a circle of rose bushes, envy

you are generous, you cling
to everything, there is no escape
from your probing soul, no way to hide
from your checklist

you even have a wand
that turns into a snake, you pretend
to be selective, we see you leaping
into the neighbor's yard, you slept

in Picasso's studio, you ate from
Lao Tzu's bowl, you died with Joan
of Arc, you rose with Jesus, you sailed
with Columbus, you ruled with the Inca

you water the plane, you rake
the leaves, you have no doubts about
the human race, it admires you, it
envies you, it clings, you see how

it has awakened to the sun, slept
under the moon, dreamed
and written many books, it makes
music driven by envy

it waits by the stream
and crosses tough roads
fending off the animals, able to
puff up with pride, to write songs

of praise, to elevate some, to downgrade
others, to make permanent decisions
on war and peace, to build hierarchies,
to establish authority, to rule politically

and culturally, to betray sunlight,
to supervise acorn. such doings
are the way of life, I sit alone
in the garden bending light

CENTURIES FULL OF WORDS

for Kevin Killian

centuries full of words and single letters
line-up on this cold evening in San Francisco's
Patagonia, we are sure nothing will do
as well as our fingers holding paper
and looking for an island,
beautiful young men demand nothing less
than a pair of elder eyes in this ancient grove
where homage is given by a breeze,
we grew old here and at nightfall hear ourselves
in the theater prone to joy,
memory shouts but we are wicked as we turn the wheel
into communion alongside flowers in their street side beds,
writing is prayer on a medieval night,
imagine the play and remember plague
find an island as dawn crumbles

there are captains with frail tin lanterns
walking tonight where ribs of the island
protrude – here you see golden dogs
from those people we admire,
we will never bring them home

BIRD SOUNDS

in memory of Kirby Doyle

the coast is alive
          bird sounds reverberate
on the spiteful ridge
Why not forgive Mount Tamalpais
   for its stern veil?

   do not blame bone-white fog
        for redwood congregations
empty the cage
        see deep into cold color
                horizon line Pacific heart —

   Kirby made us wait
he showed us an impossible temple
   of pebbles and twigs
        witness a perfect piano
   eyes of a hawk
     rising over Point Mendocino
stay calm pal, love scented air
   you see a dead rock speaking
come to understand what it means
     to feel coastal wind
   Kirby says this is my temple
        I scraped the side of my car
on the narrow road, the local kids
     threw pebbles
it was an unmitigated riot
   Kirby was taken to Laguna Honda
   way up there in paradise, you say to step out of a
comfortable beat generation, you say it's something
like
        banging on a drum, Kirby's amused life, he looked
like John Wayne —

    his temple
in the solar solitude of bush country
     steady sure breeze
         as you might find in a play –
  awaken to ashes, light is dark
 once more   I saw the lit torch hanging
   do you remember typewriters
 banging away? Kirby spoke solemnly
 where did Lew go
                     Wieners
for my birthday he gave me inscribed copy
 of *Wentley*
  Philip Lamantia and Kirby Doyle visiting
  from San Francisco
  they died, Eric hung himself in Eureka
no longer the wild child
    in a hut on the coast
  where birds warbled
   gather kindling and build
 a sacred circle
    put a hood on go to sleep
a planet filled with joyful arms
    pocketful of light
  his temple goes tumbling
   praise will o' the wisp
 of chill hill
  where one might hope to find a dove
 instead of traffic on 101

POET 2015

for Jack Mueller

1

on this ladder we scale
pathways to immortality,
we fondle books, treasure ideas
we shovel flakes on a high country driveway,
jays keel over laughing
on reckless beloved land
subversive cumulus on tap
where men live off the grid
to preen and do battle
they are who we are
in this factory of noise
built on bristlecone and spruce

be quiet like the mouse
nibbling butane tank
in an ornate town pinned onto frost

cross-country skiers
speak from the emergency ward
devoted to stealth and silence
bag of stone-faced vehemence
commanding a massive truck
wobbling ridge of cabins
nation for refugees, bighorn sheep
men who need beer breaks

2

the age of hard liquor stretches this friend
as he chases logs down to Hades
on Winter's ice box, he laughs like a child

bent stolen discarded even decimated
shadows across jingoistic ridges
where men in hunting caps
trick the doe into submission

3

body speaks to mind, image flutters kind
ruthless natural pine of weather from the line
of a wild traffic sign

to know words for seeing taking to bind
where land is thrust up dead dollar
and worm-dimes

spread your quilt on real estate
for the mountain singer-saint
moving quick brain to the threat
of morning's rain

always instinct plays
on his solitude, he whistles
on the deck, bear lumbers into sight
unnamed birds bring him strings
to venerate before the fireplace

fierce deep roar of a curated storm
she waves to a cricket from his red parka

Jack is an angel feeding the sunset's
rose-colored dues born in twisted boughs he calls at midnight:

'the blue spruce are in rebellion…"
and then his voice goes soft: "Rise, poets –
rise, break down the gate,"
and informs me there is a promissory note
levied at the moonlight, "Wait and see."

4

twice those Rocky trees
pointed to absolution for grump grandfather
of a human stump – he grumbles
and pours divine didactic lyric
into a mixing bowl of cosmic proportion

praise spruce! hug a bristlecone!
go find them in vanished
mining town with its asinine junk
for the wandering jester

ire fold delicate blossoms
mutter hello buddy
to believe your heart
in the matter of friendship
and loyalty, another pack 'o smokes
more whiskey for forwarding

in case of fire build history

5

those assembled honor tradition
though they appear to break rank
vortex holds, center maintains
dawn's cruelty bloodied sparrow

he waits in high country for good things to appear
strikes a match to keep his ass in gear

6

Jack smokes the night woods and finds delight
despite terrible truth

certain plants flourish high on the peaks,
not roses or pansies tough particles of life

toss coins before nightfall
luminous creator – drive to town
for a hot cup a brace of eggs
random morning talk round the headlines

men the size of December ramble in

savor heat and pine rust as the earthmover
moves into position twixt Iwo Jima and Telluride

the birds will themselves beyond

EAST OF AUTUMN

for Aaron Shurin

1

live for honor
and sound

   adoring church
        trees, smiling

in honor of companions?
past
embankments

a true falsehood

2

in the cold concrete cell
a world, the words
are made out of tin, the dogs
suffer, the cats remain cautious

all time
consumed
in itself

3

rain fell several hours
on Blue Cut, fell for rugged
cliff sloped along lower ridge

fell over Grapevine
onto the toes of William Blake

into the valley
of grapes and pears

4

I know we will be here
on the isolated island in
a guest house, 5 a. m.
we'll walk to the cove
and satisfy ourselves
swirling angry ocean breeze
come whipping
out of fragmented thoughts

5

the death of Maximus, not
old, rather young, who stood
in the rain forest
on the dry island, stars twinkle
in our palms, star systems die
are there innumerable galaxies
are there other universes
why do we die? why do we survive?
why do we ask when will we return?

6

we grow squash
in this area, that is why
a solid wall provides

7

awake early enough
to claim dominion over
so many thoughts, early enough
to like the idea
of the sun, sun will rise

8

leave us to live in this pretty
cottage a penny's worth
of poetry – proper song

9

you trust the Odes
because they are formed out of
the blue mist

and you weave patiently
like the master in Oaxaca
at his loom, it is dark
ever darker

10

a pocketful of rye

11

in the synapses
        echoes, dreams, fern trees
    and the barely discernible
        words of fallen scribes

12

come find a bird
and build the nest

come create a nest
and carve the tree

go be an albatross
flying off the reef

praise the bird
weathering morning's storm

"Out of the cradle
endlessly rocking..."

birdbrain

13

I was not alone
said the leather-faced
fisherman, never alone

14

he dreamt of Paris
in the sullen night

dreamt of Rimbaud
and Verlaine, the chaos

of light, inclement weather
on the quay

Notre Dame floating
above the clouds

 and on it goes
the trade-off, the simple

idea of getting past
envy, of learning control

a daffodil

15

they kill the great beasts
here in the library
where books are sucked dry
of their marrow

16

around you say echo
you say bound to be found
to see round the square
in a loop of the stream
past a Renaissance palace
good bee radiant queen
roses and red posies old
woman hobbling across
bride's memorial

17

a house for Odes
    where the Sycamore is in
the bird
    and the sky is on

the rooftop

    punish no memory

18

she was sad and
silent I added a rose
in honor of her eyes
I spoke of honor
because it is a rose

19

the flower has a soul
over the river
the river has its faults
we hope to be sublime
one day on the bluff
by a cove
sea hawks
brave articulate gold

20

the entire South Atlantic
   caught napping, snap twigs
bend a truth

      that bird is a wing –
            men learn how to sing

   "if these shadows have offended"
         then these odes are recommended

            for the just man

CARVING MERCY FROM AN ALTARPIECE

for Paul Vangelisti

1

in *Faust* I read
splinters of wood I saw
mercy yes forgetting the warp
of time all those years
sitting in Hank's living room
swilling beer
long slope
safe at last
random visions
alone in my room
off Sunset
twinkling
ding dong bell
from memory's kitchen sink

to hear Hemingway
fill the air
of a Summer's night
goodbye to
sunshine
you screwed me
one last time

the living room
is a shrine
Charles Bukowski
lived here
died elsewhere, 74 years
old, mentor, drinking
buddy

I heard it on the news
Goethe has died
Bukowski died as well

the blue bird
died and the mouse

at the end of Faust
consciousness
is purged of doubt

it is for the shorter poems
of Goethe
wreaths, arbors
and animals
and a country road

or to be lifted
out of the naive tongue
crawling through perfect
German nouns
where lawns crystalize
so swell tank half empty
the main thing
is to surrender
to culture
nailed into letters
of each word

großer Dichter

"in the shadow of the rose"

2

no remedy
for stupidity
a sense of unity
for maternity

I've been suffering
an Israelite in my hair
I shed no tears

so realize each petal
as you might a Ming vase
over green façades
of the sad human race

that good reigns
like rain rains
over statues in
your cerebral dead

bake fine bread for sleeping men
who have written paradise
for Lucifer's table
and trust no man

3

we thank your mother's house
west of Parma
not quite to the white spire
of Carrara's flawless stone,
a propane life
and liquor from the gods
who settle on tree branches

there's more yeast
in the story so sorry
for a grid of animosities
baked out of the adobe
or somber tar pits
young fragile
ambitious nerves

propelled to soar
on the Arroyo Seco Freeway

and Big John Thomas
sailing to Patagonia
with memories of
the madhouse
visiting Ezra and a paean
for Stravinsky

Ezra watched
the squirrels
but unclean toilets
of grandeur
took his strength away

this is not a voyage
to be inflicted on men
in their studios writing
verse

4

carving mercy from
an altarpiece for a box
of Asian Odes

I find you
in the late afternoon
among lupine
and coastal oak
casting a line
into the river
as it flows

KNOWING JESSICA

if you do not know Jessica Loos
then you are missing New York City
San Francisco
Spec's Bar on Columbus Avenue
across from City Lights Books
tall, elder eyes
of Jack Hirschman
the memory of Harvey Silver
and clover and hard
liquor and wine
boys at the bar
and her tambourine

I'm not kidding
the old ways yes old trails
of Manhattan last living
eruption from beast from
sweet generation from devil
in imagination from reliable
Mrs. Satan (yet again) yes
she bubbles up she rises
out of miasma out of sanitary crap
of Microsoft Bird yes you can

yes you can take back words
sweetheart you must try to see
simple prison block
death camps golden future
the mean heart mean eyes
be like a panda munching bamboo
or a herd of elephants nibbling grass

I see Jessica
she comes for Christmas lunch
and gives my house a lift
into the bedazzling canopy of stars

ANTLER AT SEVENTY

the worst weather is in my head
I want to tell you
now that you are an elder poet
up in that north land

you see now it isn't all bad
nor sweet, your life
has been poetry continued
through Autumn's gracious reign

the usual leaves turn into ice cream cones
their veins are chocolate capillaries
when I examine them,
maybe you know more than what I see

up there closer to the woods,
bear with me, Antler, through peonies
and greeneries, through the deaths
of our beloved friends,

it was supposed to be simpler,
spring and those posies
in the nursery rhyme, we
fall and cross our hearts

a pocketful of inclement weather
tickles our backs, every sentence
memorable, words, woods,
we fall and fly away

SHOSTAKOVICH ON THE RADIO

way back then we'd gather, you and I
with Rachmaninoff, Sibelius, and Mahler,
they would rise out of the radio on a side table
near the couch that smelled like a dead cat

you like those guys, "tough old men"
you called them, the grave-toned masters
who drew despair over Hollywood's happy endings –
"The human voice ruins
the music," Mahler struck like thunder
on De Longpre Avenue

I remember cases of Miller's Beer
and a toast to the gods of music,
you knew their lives,
talked of them; one evening
as Dimitri Shostakovich rose,
out of one of the last symphonies,
it rained, a loud L.A. deluge,
the kind that never stops,
it keeps pouring even when we're old and gray

we were glorious smoking cheap
cigars from Ned's Liquors, and the
Russian composer battled it out
with duels and death, "He's
a God," you said, the music
pushing and pulling

then it was forty-two years later,
the apartment now a city landmark,
in memory – your typewriter and
radio, I'm attending an opening reception
in your honor at the Huntington Library
in San Marino

the bartender hands
me a diet coke, I tell him,
"Bukowski and I used to drink beer
four days in a row while
listening to music," he
responds, "Who is Bukowski?"

I looked at the display cases
of letters, manuscripts,
and books, and photographs
on the wall...

One night Shostakovich
visited while we
drank to excess, he chain-
smoked and bit his nails,
when the music ran wild
he turned into a furnace
and we drank

that was life back in 1969
more or less, now it's a bit
more tame, you are at peace
under a filthy rug, the libraries
are stainless, book bindings stink

we are lost on a dung-heap
in the library with Chaucer
and Shakespeare,
Shostakovich still sells, maybe
not like in the old days,
but times change
as must our music and the muse

DONG KINGMAN

    Yes, Dong, you remain a faded graph

    painted figures coming out of a fog bank
on Montgomery Street in a watercolor from 1941

    ought to surprise no one   in the dirty air Pearl Harbor

you were chased
        for being "The Enemy," but you were Hong Kong
born your pal picked up a block of wood
    and hit a guy over the head, then you both ran
down Hotaling Place… "I kicked the shit out of him
when he came up from around the corner,"

        we were in the Li Po, Bobby Kaufman and me,
    in the Li Po Bar drinking 'em down, Bobby lived with me, I'd make
dinner every night and usually had to throw it into the garbage
        as Bobby died and fell into the Bay, we said goodbye
    ash by ash from a box we held over
his head, our little wind-up rebel saint
                with his strong mind, the black saint

from New Orleans, those eloquent sisters
    who showed up
        for so many John F. Kennedy
    conspiracy theories, sisters of our
bard who wrote, "o man in inner basement core
of me…" as if there was only one jazz club
    and as if this planet was Chinatown
on an alley of blood and guts

    lights are low, there's Chinatown and there's
the angel, there's the ship of good luck
        and a harbor filled with death, a Chinese testament,
        a hopeful world, a need to be real
a need for the ruckus to end –
                little overt push for love

little light, beautiful rightness, terrific wisdom
of the baker and butcher, terrific

    arrogance of an artist late at night

Bobby Kaufman's China poems his disappearance
during the Cultural Revolution
    when the thing to do was to take a pair of
        scissors and cut up a poet's scroll, or a sledge hammer
            and send some ancient pottery to smithereens
                or a wise grandmother to re-education camp
in the far country, mid-Winter

like that, everyone with balls
    had a chance in our world of lanterns

        the *Odes* stand like monoliths, the *Analects* offer
            a route to order, the *Tao* keeps the mind free, and the *I Ching*
advises, it's not always black and white,
            not forever north or south

        those anonymous men
in the Li Po, leaping, drinking, matching one
    another, drink for drink

    it's not just Chinatown, it's a chime
        and one last parking spot
        in Pearl Harbor when you and Sam
                faded into photographs
and memories, into old watercolors

WALKING IN BERLIN

for Alan Kaufman

boundaries were gone
and the Wall, gone, so we walked
along *Unter Den Linden*
in the late morning
past the restoration leaves
and pages of the trees, I was wrong
in thinking there would be no end
to the series of grand palaces,
and you would go on to write *Jew Boy*
in another world, the blocks in the Bronx
rushing through your veins,
I would rage wishing the trees would forever guard
my coming and going,
we walked was enough, finally, as
an elderly couple passed fleeing the
advancing Russians, and four rabbinical
students dropped out of a cloud
speaking the dialect of Berlin, and
we were sequestered in an airplane
over Iceland, do you remember?
ah, *Unter Den Linden,* caged and
roaring, taken under the wings
of German poets, we came to read
our journals, we made memorable advances
over the farmland and on
screaming teeming *Autobahn* in
a van and we walked
along *Unter Den Linden*
through impressive tomes of loom
and flowers, we knew
just where to step, just how to smile
and when to acknowledge
the fields of ghosts, and how to
turn the screw so the sun would emerge
ever more anonymously profound

oh we were set free, so sublime,
free of error, middle aged
average age of a universe is what?
do you think perhaps 40 billion years
give or take a few? does it matter
when dizzy doers walk and
walk and walk and think
silent thoughts, and share a
thought or two on the avenue
flanked by ponderous gray
monuments to folk rituals and
shaman dreams, to the many-headed
demons and angry hungry dragons

we are dizzy walking
it never ends, two of us, just us,
and behind our bodies dust and ash, and in front
signs of division, markings
of revenge, in our heads
who knows? in the palaces
the time-tested has given way to the new,
you need to re-invent,
you need to change,
you must erase the organisms
that clink and cut you to pieces
and shatter your sense of freedom

GREGORY CORSO

when Gregory dies
there is a white butterfly
in the yard taking notes
and talking to the lemon tree
in a low and antique voice

when Gregory dies
the piano players take a bow
in the yard next door
on the day of graduation
and a lone piccolo preaches
to anyone passing

he was born in 1930
in time for the Great Depression
and was passed from
one strange hand to another
he did not know his mother

**

I met Gregory on Columbus Avenue
with the poet Andy Clausen
the hod carrier, they came to my apartment
and I read my "Coit Tower" poem in which
the tower is a shadow folded
over a bed of flowers while the sky leaks
and the streets turns into a series of laundries

he had his own "Coit" poem
in a book called *Gasoline*
an anti-vertiginous tower
which struck me as defiance

**

he may have been one of the last bohemian poets
no MFA, no university job, no job at all
except poesy

while he lived and worked
snow fell over his words,
sunlight bore
into his poems, wolves leapt
every chance they had
when he'd turn his neck
to the skylarks escaping
the grip of Shelley,
his master, the always young poet
who wept for the dead

**

when Gregory was
a demonic Huck Finn
he learned how to
proceed along
zigzag path, in prison
he was handed poetry
and illuminated prose

when he was freed
everything moved poetically
on Greenwich Village's
hometown morning streets and
in the Harvard neighborhoods
where he made his
first book of poems

**

when I met Gregory
he was already a famous poet
of the Beat Generation, he could
quote Poe's "To Helen" and
celebrate "the agate lamp"

Gregory wrote "Marriage"
and "Bomb," he stole my
stereo for drug money,
he left baby Max under my
care for weeks at a time

he spoke of Francois Villon
as if he were a brother, not
a medieval poet of the
dark Parisian colonnades

**

when Gregory lives
a marching band
rises from the garden
and assumes control
of all that is neat

he kept us writhing
for his light, he thought
our country oversimplified
and found a complete
complex of simplicity
in a few well-chosen lines

HYDRA WATERFRONT

in memory of Harold Norse

yes the water is perfect and
still, the Flying Dolphin
skids on the Gulf and slow
only moments before entering
the harbor and gliding
to the waterfront, it's a rugged
land of rocks and whitewashed
facades

on Ὑδρα the Venetian
palaces give supplication
to Helios, Jackie O visited
while I was there, and
your pal Leonard Cohen
saw "a bird on a wire" which
landed in a song, there was
the British expatriate who
painted his way
into an alcoholic
dream...

no, I haven't been there
for seven years, and you
were put into a home
in Hayes Valley, assigned
to a room that looks
out on a tree
and you lived to wander,
the attendants took care
to meet your needs

I'd come to see you
in advanced age,
eyes shining and
poems burning up
in a drawer, we had to
walk the waterfront
and feel the breeze

on Ὑδρα once
I made love to a
young man from
Salonika, (Hal, he had
dark, hairy legs).
we spent five days
in a room
by the port, the chubby
matron who brought
us food would giggle,
knowing...

I loved your poems
about every Ὑδρα
sprinkled over
many lands,
your shades of
sensibility flowing
on the wharf, awake
like a seabird
cawing at the action
on the waterfront

you told me
about the donkey boy
who was hung
like a horse, was
he the wizened
old man
I saw gathering
memories on the
stone pier jutting into
the harbor?

I miss you
more than I miss
you, I guess it is

a love without
measure, you
were the man
who showed me
at least one way
out of solitude
and back to the self

I picture you
on Ὕδρα
in the 50s, sitting
poised to write
of the people
below your window
the donkeys braying,
crowds milling
across the water
in the harbor over time
to those catacombs
below the poem

FOR AGNETA FALK

of late a sun
walks over the hill
and settles-in

bright light on
yellow facades
face the workroom

you're singing in Swedish –
clear air whispers an elder
song so elderly
it defies humanity, we
must go, we need to
jump, no choice

you sing in the native
tongue, the sun
trickles through dawn's
taut riggings, aligns wily
wily wounds, I imagine
you, across town,
another sun or a part
of this one by your window
looking out on the Bay

you've made coffee already,
you're smoking a cigarette,
the nightingales are
somewhere else, all storms
overseas, we travel
through the Passage, day by day

THE POET IS NOT A PRIEST

for Jerome Rothenberg

the poet takes time out to call
till human voices turn into wood
I'll take redwood, aspen will also do
or sandalwood from a Balinese dream

the poet places incense in a jar
trees kick him, turn branches
toward life-giving flames,
the poet enjoys flowers below deck

he knows mynah birds,
he wonders who paints them
why do crows squawk
on unsuspecting telephone poles

the poet wants to fly to the sparrow
who must attend the university
in this world of war machines
because fledglings will sing of dust

the poet is not a priest
he follows river blood over slick
black boulders and builds
an imaginary blanket of white water

fragile twigs rule the universe,
my Lord preserves sanctity –
flowers bellow in a meadow's groin

the poet is not a priest
(oh yes he is says the marble-throated
blue bird bathing by the creek)

as folks continue to struggle
colors demand notice
Rumi dances – Aswan cracks – the circus
creates a circle on hard soil –

I need a pear orchard
and a luscious ripe pear –
the poet is a shaman
come up from the tribe

POET 2016

for Tate Swindell

I claim endurance

it had something to do
with serving creation
serving grass and trees
lambs and lions, embracing
crucified mobster of freedom

yeah, suddenly I unconcealed
nettles at the beginning of comprehension

I hopped like a jackrabbit
on an infested field
the Faerie Queen
wore torn jeans
she showed-off smug tattoos

poetry is shrouded
in everything nice, when the poet
is born he has a sugar ration
card, an old blue Ford
with running boards
a president named Harry Truman
packages of tears
from the concentration camps

the poet chug-a-lugs uphill
like a train, he blows his whistle, he
sinks teeth into wrecked concrete
built on ice, he is a pee-stained
septuagenarian who favors
wrenching letters dumbstruck
under the thumb
of a hard-driving rain shower

a dog with a bad attitude
has been hired to sweep the stairwell
and prove other traumatic
cosmic connections bound by
the rules of science, say hello
to the improvised god and
goodbye to the wasteland

JACK KEROUAC

I'd rather get on a plane
and travel to Paris or disappear in Mexico, I sit
in the garden growing old,
I read *Mexico City Blues*
perplexed, wondering
why words we speak are made to bend
out of shape, why Jack Kerouac
still sells in a nation grown dour, why people
who study writing generally read
more careful work, they see
professionalism as a goal,
I see writing as a pool
of water rippling to shore

I stand by that water, it is cold,
colors collide
and become one conspiratorial force
that brings
a sense of mortality into focus,
I see sentimentality
buried in the poem, I must trim
Kerouac's prose, to forget
the excess, to embrace
a celebration of empty places
to jumpstart verbs
across the pages, to retake the fortress
of a spooky death, his angel brother,
an early death, his own
in a barrage of alcohol,
and to be not quite so quick
condemning men who venture
onto the field

I'd rather open my notebook
to a rhododendron grove
where enemies live,
I cast on the dry
dusty ground, it's so good
to be assessed by silence, okay to be told
what not to do by a god who walks
in my brain, to trim
the hedges of my notebook
until the sun is a copper penny, so fine
to let words lead the mind
as if they were amulets
forged by a shaman who believes
in the animal he wears on his head;
I digested the *Blues*
a book Jack wrote
long ago, pious, profane
improvisations
credited to rhythms
we often deny
on our way to the forge.

ARTHUR RIMBAUD

in memory of Eric Walker

push elegies toward a final pen
as solitude
spreads over vineyards
north of town
the migratory billboards
announce imprisoned acrobat
of the apocalypse

this year the snow pack
promises a record melt
I won't count on it
until my feet are buried
in the blue blazes
of your blond arms

late in 1961 I brought
a red and yellow collection
of Rimbaud and ambled
to the wash over Highland Avenue
on my way to school

I used to smile at the woodblocks
and memorize certain lines, the seven
year old poet explodes, the traveling
bard floats on a river of red men

he is a chubby woodblock
who tumbles onto rough terrain
fingered by a truant officer
delivered to Doctor Bailey's office

gracias for traps that helped
loosen shackles, screw you, asshole
I own these poems

it wasn't that I noticed
or gave a damn, just
simply sheets of snow
fell over my eyes
under boughs of sycamore
I counted innumerable horses
an occasional fat rat
I memorized his explosive lines
and the opening to
a portrait of the dead wilderness

men came out of their houses
in three-wheeled carts
to pick up medical marijuana
at the roadside
and Mexico crawled over
a grim border

we read and find so much
amiss, calculations
remain unconnected

now in a painting by
Paul Gauguin I see Arthur Rimbaud
rising over Tahiti

poor Paul Verlaine
whimpering beautiful French phrases
kaput!

Rimbaud mad advances
in my adolescent head

I walked up Perris Hill Park
on a ruthless noon

we heard school bells
folded into a Peter Pauper Press
edition of the poems, it was as if
the barbarians had done
a terrific job illustrating his ripe cheeks
and wild hair

we have only obscure
photos of his renunciation
and as for "terrible" it trembles
past the psycho-pathology of
the French Republic

as usual things
fall apart, might as well
be buried under the ash
of a distant idea

I kept those poems
through my eternal years,
no one could rob me of the young
Frenchman, nor explain his
down-going, nor steal his Arabian
nights, the secret in his unwritten
epic of empty shores

remain content
as if the spirit meant everything it said
both in dream and in
the real world

BUDDHA

for Gary Gach

        nothing has changed
in this burial place, one of the spots
    where Buddha lies,
only you have changed, your eyes
are made of mulberries, great stupas
    shine in the sun

    keep changing
and remain surprised –
        you must understand what happened
        before Buddha became Buddha

when he was an aristocrat
 in a house of marble

*

        you need to see the night sky
    as he saw it, stop
complaining and accept
    riches pouring down
        from a secret chest

  bare the hostility
        of oak trees   cease praising
    your entrepreneurial soul

    lest the Tempter hurls thoughtfulness
        into a shadowed pit

*

        dew rests at the foot
of supine Buddha

        hamadryads flirt with
            white rose petals

        gather reddish hue in late flowering

    *

        Buddha's remains are flown
        from house to house   prayers
            are sown like wheat   women wail
            and men perish   soldiers swarm
                the barricades   play chess
until the bishop
    is down on his knees

        sleep until sun rays knocks loudly
on the Venetian blinds
        and sketch a composition

GREAT BASIN SUTRA

1

I followed Philip Whalen
   from the Zen Center

"Oh My My well gosh and golly..."

folded quilt like sheets
                         temple bells ring
            – cleanse your arms
                  bathe
as the Basin rolls – Amtrak bellows
      tossed by junkyard

            twenty battered bikes
                              sound nearby states
         hello sleepers!

oh those minds, he went up Sourdough Peak
            with pancake mix and Heraclitus

   Buddha bounces

two hunters
   going after the cougar

                              beautiful hawk
      famous eagle – mustangs, allowed to be wild, the elk
         standing on the sky

               we learn
                  to hold the diamond upright
amusing smoke rushes over
         the rise, alters plummet, bones squint
archives frown, this shit-hole town

   grocers come out of their caves to witness
               a fine block of fumes,
         gasoline leaks

                    we never held a revolver up
                to the authorities of sleep
        nor did we say "This is a cemetery"
                except beneath breathing eyes,
            discrete difficulties
                are hot coals burning through
glamor, they make holes
                    in our thinking, ruin the still life
                        paintings, we're calm participants
though we rave, and identify our foe

                our fine pronouncements
                    go up in smoke, we say "Fuck this"
                and "Fuck that" until we
                        are lost in lack of meaning

        Whalen and I go calmly to the Buddhist Center
        in the days of auto dealerships

            the British Empire
        brought the Pāli to our hands

    2

you must toss the cat out the window
            and let her land on a drawbridge

            braving morning breeze
            chipmunks gathering food
                let rabbits embrace
we will be surprised

doesn't everyone's grandmother
come from the former Soviet Union
and light Friday candles,
hands cupped safely above the flames

we know ravens
who roost on a stick

    now you fill paper
with crows and robin red-breast
occasionally daubing grasshoppers

        words are stored on a magic slate

        early every morning
                life rises in Winter's variety shop

here we find Jabberwocky hard at work

        every poem should begin on your fingertip
          the very ground of being
    volumes of night
           miles of gasoline, train track
on a forehead, bells ringing over a fence of strawberries

    from these doubts rise massive cows—
inches of hillside not an obstruction, now one
carves into the high juniper as do the priests
who belong to the wolf clan

**

      save some boyhood
as you tear down the decades
leave a trace of the lake, let the fox
prepare a table, celebrate clouds
surrounded by rare objects, careful to
water plants   when multitudes
are silenced by starvation you will be alone

**

I wait for the wildcat in the land of limestone
do you doubt? are you awake
or is this locomotive streaming into your brain?

                    Winter cats perform daily rituals
         be able to struggle out of the pale

**

         father came from the eagle's lair
     he did not free you from dangerous Alpine
sentences

    where men disappear, whorl
        of freedom's echo

how do elk horns sound
    once the orchestra goes
        on strike?

AN ELEGY FOR FRANK O'HARA (1978)

and that trees whisper green in brown bark
while redwoods become victims of the one world government
and Frank you wouldn't know any of this the way it is
in my three room place confidentially
wounded by self and selfish
or that the problem with me is that I always ask questions
even if these cafes are not Paris and I don't know the elegant song
trapped inside my body unable to arise
but last night I saw San Francisco from the ferry boat to Sausalito
1970s downtown towers and 30s Coit Tower Telegraph Hill
and thought how good to know a place and be in it
not merely on top but actually un-alienated returning
from several weeks away realizing how the geography
is a friendly pat on the back or a couple of hands on the shoulders
or that we do not meet people accidentally it is a plan
and that my old love and I may not know
I wonder why you never came here finally I am
still on the ferry boat crossing to Sausalito in gray black fog
one light on Alcatraz famous ghost
o dear everyone we see weeds waiting on lots
outside of town on trolley cars and trains
with their own aching desires
and to you dead now many years
why you actually wrote things down like I am doing
I read these things and cannot stop complaining
but memorialize the past on Sausalito ferry boat
the lynx of machinery in water

WILD WEST

On a pre-historic mountainside
            the monk of ten thousand songs
    battles demons, some of whom choke on thunderstorms –
            the one I approach owns a gold Mercedes –

he forgives confusion in the brotherhood
            we pass Heartbreak Hotel and
                    enter a snow shed, promises I keep
go down to synagogues,
    my brothers scramble
as darkness offers light, earth crumbles
we emerge, blankets of snow bespeak desire,
I summon reserve strength and feel smooth walls
            of chaotic chambers

    artful and spirited, wise in the ways
of all demons the wild one devours road signs
            and broods over real estate

he wears a red scarf, a battered Stetson and drinks his fill
    in the bar

        *

            I draw water from the creek
boil it over an open campfire, coffee is
            indescribably fine, I sip, I wait, mosquitos
pass, my notebook summons heat
now left behind

        night creatures attend mass
mice on the roof keep me up,
            wood is consumed, ashes
            turn bone-white
    one ivory speck of ash fragile bee
            flying upside-down

        *

I salute my generation
                when we sprinkle ashes
of those whom we love

  in morning breeze I read of birth and death,
of selfishness and decay, of beautiful martyrs
    who keep sane, flame into ash, shadow into light

    Jimmy Broughton
        film-maker, poet, friend would
                gently hold my hand, his remains
        sailing onto afternoon water from brown box

*

    David Meltzer listens to Milky Way
soliloquies and says, "Neeli, you are becoming
                the Jewish Gary Snyder"

        enamored of damp morning hills
            precipitous cliffs and the odor of bear shit

    I walk to the outhouse
        after a long spin on Bixby Beach

            truth is not simple, it holds yellow-tipped irises
        and offers them to travelers on the Zephyr

*

fly over fine white sand
        land on dunes, if you go inland
find home fries and biscuits

comes Art Goodtimes in long gray beard
to re-arrange priorities in the country of Green
evolution – badger bows

poppa, oh pop
do not die, my hands hold sacred
rattlers, the sun hisses
and sends a river onto parched butte

sober snakes pinch the mesa

cougar on divide awaiting traffic lights to change
before crossing

BLUE SPLENDOR

blue splendor
still captivates
past ink stains
and stressed syllables

will the prophets
ordain a song
in this fragile Neptune
and hit pavement
leading to alchemy

I'd trade grammar
for another few seconds
of your warm body
pressed against quiet beatitude

I offer a chest of
brittle leaves
in dazed precincts

I stare at eternal sleep
and take the thorns
off your brow

I saw you
leaving the publishing house
for private pursuits, what connections
burn? do we touch
our lost children
and turn them into flares?

solitude sprints
to dangerous cliffs
where your blonde hair
remains a medallion
I may cherish
as ashes of light
make love
to the swells

JOANNE KYGER

I must go home
before nightfall, the road is
difficult enough and
Joanne is gone

I need to leave
right now, this land of spiders
and weathered barns
is alien, I took the wrong road
Joanne is gone

there will be storms
Buddha bonds littered
on sand
music from the Chinese
marching band
strange branches on
handsome trees
withered or fiercely intact
Joanne is gone

are we all army brats
grown into men and women
despite the traffic
and border guards? I hear
the sea less than 40 meters away
and must needs pray
for silence at the end of the rope
because so many of us
turn to the late light
on Mount Tamalpais
across the mesa
Joanne is gone

the earth belongs
to the poet
she made that clear
in concise terms, we turn

to hear a lizard on paper
firefly at midnight
in a temple of skies
and trims the rocks
until they shed tears
Joanne is gone

the poet is near to all animals:
"that the ants seem to wobble
as the morning sun
catches their shadow…"

but for the moment it is late
and we drive home
Joanne is gone

WHAT'S IN AN ELEGY?

you'll find the wisdom of Timbuktu
in the elegy, a Persian cat will jump
from the mirror and extend one paw
because she is talking, she hugs you
she knows you honor the feline banner

you'll encounter the beekeeper
who listens to the rising sun, urns of olive oil
will be transported by ship,
Sumerian dreamers ask for courage

in the elegy your mouth and my tongue
your belly button, the circus will come to town
with its trapeze show, a map of Istanbul
will overtake smiling silences –
calm seas and sunflowers
of Vincent van Gogh may amuse

In the elegy I read Neruda and Rimbaud
and sleep in Homer's palm, puppet dreams become
life dreams, Huckleberry Finn swings in the wind
down the Mississippi, my river is a wall
of light, oh my Lord lives elegiacally

what's in an elegy? you'll find cockle-shells
a busted doorbell, clogged drainpipe
sacred plumbing, much to savor
and consider, come to the feast of Buenos Aires
and the funeral of a ceremonial cat

the elegy will show you mirrors
take a lot of effort, you don't wear
a dunce cap, in the elegy are numerous
birds, plenty of foot-soldiers, we want
to explore, we are born for elegiac words

there is a "yes" and a "no," you'll find
damnation or redemption, it depends
on state of mind, many acacia trees
in the park, green benches await
unbridled freedom provides a song

Neeli Cherkovski is the author of many books of poetry, including *From the Canyon Outward* (2009), and *The Crow and I* (2015). He was the coeditor of *Anthology of L.A. Poets* (with Charles Bukowski) and *Cross-Strokes: Poetry between Los Angeles and San Francisco*. Cherkovski also wrote biographies of Lawrence Ferlinghetti and Charles Bukowski, as well as the critical memoir *Whitman's Wild Children* (1988). His papers are held at the Bancroft Library, University of California, Berkeley. He has lived in San Francisco since 1974.

Author's Note:

My special thanks to George Scrivani for his editorial
work on the manuscript, as well as to Danny Rosen and
Kyle Harvey of Lithic Press for their efforts.

BOOKS BY NEELI CHERKOVSKI

POETRY

Poems for the Wailing Wall (1968)

Pre-Rabbinic Poems (1969)

Don't Make a Move (1973)

The Waters Reborn (1975)

Public Notice (1975)

Love Proof (1980)

Home, American (1983)

Juggler Within (1983)

Animal (1996)

Elegy for Bob Kaufman (1996)

Leaning Against Time (2004)

A Packet of Love Poems (2008)

From the Canyon Outward (2009)

From the Middle Woods (2011)

Mania Poems (2013)

The Crow and I (2015)

PROSE

Ferlinghetti: A Biography (1979)

Whitman's Wild Children (1988, 1998)

Hank: The Life of Charles Bukowski (1991, also
published in a revised edition as
Bukowski: A Life in 1997)

EDITOR

Anthology of L.A. Poets (1972, co-edited with
Charles Bukowski and Paul Vangelisti)

Peace or Perish: A Crises Anthology (1983, co-edited
with Herman Berlandt)

*Cross Strokes: Poetry Between Los Angeles
and San Francisco* (2015, co-edited with Bill Mohr)

Collected Poems of Bob Kaufman (forthcoming,
edited with Raymond Foye and Tate Swindel)